Alien Invasions

Thrillogy

Edited by Paul Collins and Meredith Costain

 sundance

Read all of the
 Titles

Fantasy/Horror	Science Fiction
Dragon Tales	Alien Invasions
Ghosts and Ghoulies	Gadgets and Gizmos
Heroic Feats	It Came from the Lab . . .
Last Gasps	Lost in Space
Tales from Beyond	Techno Terror
Terrors of Nature	Time Zones

Published by Sundance Publishing
P.O. Box 1326, 234 Taylor Street, Littleton, MA 01460

Copyright in individual stories remains with the authors.

First published 1999 as Spinouts by
Addison Wesley Longman Australia Pty Limited
95 Coventry Street, South Melbourne 3205 Australia
Exclusive United States Distribution: Sundance Publishing

ISBN 0-7608-4830-0

Printed in China

Contents

The Mine 5
Kerry Greenwood 6
(From an idea by David Butcher)

Cressy's Friend 19
Lucy Sussex 20

So Sorry! 33
Shannah Jay 34

The
Mine

The author
Kerry Greenwood
talks about the story

"I was having a deep conversation with my highly intelligent nephew, David Butcher, and he wondered what would happen next. He also drew a picture of a monster—a gigantic caterpillar. I also wanted to know what would happen next, so I wrote the story to find out."

The Mine

"What should we do now?" asked Matthew.

"What else is there to do?" asked David.

"Too rainy for baseball," said Matthew. "And we finished the jigsaw puzzle and the TV's broken."

David had come to stay with his cousin Matthew a few days before and was beginning to miss his hometown, where it was never too rainy to do something.

"What else is there to see?"

"Well, there's the mine," said Matthew. "You can see the entrance from here."

David saw a square hole in the side of the mountain.

"Can you lend me a raincoat?" he asked.

"No, we can't go there. It's dangerous!"

"And I'm bored," said David.

The house contained many things, including Matthew's chemistry set, but no extra raincoat.

Matthew wore a yellow raincoat, and David made do with a trash bag.

"Why do we need matches?"

"It's dark in the mine," explained Matthew.

They stood at the entrance. Cold air breathed forth. Matthew lit two torches. David saw his cousin's face, skull-like, in the strange light. He swallowed. Maybe this was not a good idea.

"Come on," he said. I'd rather be dead than bored was his motto.

"The mine's on three levels," said Matthew. "This is the elevator. You pull on the rope and you go up."

"Why did they close this mine?"

"Dad said some people got killed, a long time ago. They saw lights in the sky, UFOs. Dad said there were three, hovering over this mountain. Then two flew away and there was a huge explosion. It made a crater."

"What killed the miners?" David asked.

"They were crushed. By rockfall, the cops said, but it wasn't. People say they heard a thumping sound, a noise like rabbits running underground."

"Are you going first?" asked David.

"All right," said Matthew. "I'll be on Level 2. See you there!"

The machinery clanked. David heard the cage stop, then pulled on the rope to bring it down. He climbed in and heard the counterbalance whir as he rose. He expected to see Matthew's light when he came up through the floor to Level 2. But Matthew's light was not there, and neither was Matthew.

"Matthew!" called David. He backed up, touching the wall. He stared at the green slime covering his palm, then wiped his hand on a clean patch of wall, shivering.

The slime wasn't cold. It was as warm as blood.

Where was Matthew?

He called again. He strained his eyes for a glimpse of light. He knew there was a whole mountain overhead, hundreds of tons of stone pressing down on the mine.

Then he heard a sound.

"Matthew?" he called hopefully.

There was a fluttering noise, like a moth trapped in a glass jar. Then he heard a thudding—like a beating heart, like rabbits under the ground.

Matthew had waited for David at the elevator on Level 3. Overshooting the second level, he'd called to David, but got no answer. So he'd walked into the tunnel.

Matthew heard a strange sound, a scratching, harsh noise that grated on his nerves. It seemed to be coming from behind, but when he turned, it throbbed in the wall beside him.

Matthew backed toward the elevator. A roar and a gush of flame filled the tunnel. There was a wave of intense heat. He couldn't see or breathe.

He pulled the elevator up quickly, jumped into it and dropped. As he sank down, he caught a glimpse of something green, glowing, and very big.

At the same time, he noticed a strange, bitter smell, like something from his chemistry set.

David heard the elevator coming down and ran to it. "There's something coming!" Matthew screamed, and David jumped into the cage with him.

A blast of heat washed over them. David saw that the back of Matthew's yellow raincoat was melted.

"It breathes fire," gasped Matthew. "What is it?"

"Do we care?" yelled David.

The thudding beat was loud. The sharp smell was choking them. The rickety elevator finally clanked to the bottom, and they yanked at the gate.

It was stuck.

"You pull, I'll push," yelled David. The noise was all around them. Like feet, David thought, like lots of feet. Was it one creature or an army of them? The roar had teeth in it. They rattled at the stubborn gate until they finally got it opened. As they leaped out, the creature roared again, and they covered their ears.

"It's down here and around one corner," yelled David. They ran blindly, stumbling over broken things on the floor, their hands covered with warm, green slime. Then they reached the corner, burst through the flimsy, wooden fence, and fell out into daylight.

"I'll never be bored again," said David. "I'll never, never be bored again." The valley was quiet. They crouched on the ground, breathless with relief.

"It nearly got us," panted David.

"I told you it was dangerous!" said Matthew, examining the melted spot on his raincoat. "Are you hurt?"

"No. Just scared out of my wits."

"That's okay." said Matthew.

"Well, we got away," concluded David.

Then they heard a sound behind them. It was the sound of feet, lots of feet.

They reached the house after a frantic scramble up

the side of the hill. Matthew found his father's backpack and began shoving clothes into it. "As soon as it gets light tomorrow, we're out of here," he said. "It's no use leaving now. I don't want to be wandering around the hills in the dark with that thing loose."

"It won't leave the mine," said David. "It lives in the mine. We just annoyed it by going in."

"Did you see it?"

"No."

"It's green, and it glows, and it spits fire—and it's big. It filled up the tunnel, and the tunnel is ten feet high."

They sat on the porch and watched the entrance to the mine. Nothing was moving. The opening was a black square in the green grass.

"See? Nothing," said David.

Behind the house, bigger than the house, the creature towered. It was covered in slime. Three orange eyes glared down at them, and a beaklike mouth clicked. Its body looked soft, green, and shining. Six suckered legs waved freely in the air.

It stank. Its smell was a weapon. Matthew jumped up and ran into the house, followed by David. "I've got an idea!" he yelled.

13

Matthew seized a bottle from the table, emptied a packet of white powder into it, and filled it with water. He shook the bottle frantically, hearing his own heart beat faster. Then he ran outside again, ducking close to the green body and flinging the contents of the bottle onto the soft flesh of the creature's underbelly.

The creature howled, rocked a little, and spat. A stream of acid, which caught fire as it flew, licked the stone house and burned off moss and cracked stone.

"Terrific, now you've made it mad!" yelled David. They dived into the house. Matthew hauled two buckets out of the kitchen and filled them with water.

"What are you doing?" asked David.

"The creature's all acid," called Matthew. "So baking soda burned it. If we get enough base maybe we can persuade it to go away."

"Base? Oh, yes, the opposite of acid. Well, okay," said David. "You think it will work?"

"Got a better idea?"

They slipped out of the house. The creature was looming over the house, its sucker feet knocking off tiles. Carrying the buckets, they staggered to the nearest part of the creature and flung the fluid over it.

The shriek knocked them both over. There was a blast of fire, then a scream that shattered all of the windows and made the ground shake. Then they heard the thudding noise again, fading as the creature retreated.

"Are you alive?" asked David from the ground.

"Yes, are you?"

"Yes." They sat up. They were bruised and slimed and singed.

"Where's the monster?"

"It went back into the mine. Isn't it lucky," said Matthew, "that Dad bought me that chemistry set last Christmas?"

"What was in the buckets?"

"Drain cleaner. It's a base."

They went inside and sat down to recover. A trail of burned grass led from behind the house down the hill to the mine. A thin trail of smoke rose from the entrance. It all looked safe.

"We did it," said David.

At three in the morning, David was woken up by a light. He dragged Matthew out to the porch. The mine was blazing with a cold, green glow.

"Maybe it's coming back," whispered Matthew. "And we don't have any more drain cleaner."

"Look!"

With a grating noise that sounded like old machinery, the top of the mountain slid slowly sideways. The boys held their breath. A green column of light poured straight up into the sky.

Gracefully and effortlessly, three vast creatures rose through the cavern, up into the light. They were gleaming silver with fragile wings and long antennae. As the boys watched, they spun around faster and faster, throwing out long strands of silverlike wire. There was a humming sound like in a hive of bees. It was hard to see through the light, but they seemed to be spinning themselves a flat, silvery covering and glowing from within.

Suddenly, all of the lights in Matthew's house went out. The radio switched channels at random, blurring through country music and news, and then died.

The creatures flew higher. They hung for a moment in the column of light. Then the light blinked out, and the mountain top noisily replaced itself.

"Look!" cried David.

The three silver creatures hung over Matthew's house, bleaching the moonlight. The boys sat frozen under the lights like deer in headlights. They had nowhere to run.

The first creature lifted, tilted, and was gone. The others followed. The night was dark again.

The radio and all of the lights in Matthew's house came on at once.

"They're like caterpillars, except that they spit acid," said David into the comforting noise. "Phosphorus makes that green light, and it burns all by itself, like that fire did. That monster, it was a caterpillar. A really, *really* big caterpillar. Caterpillars grow until they turn into moths."

"Those were the biggest moths ever," said Matthew. "So I guess they had to be the biggest caterpillars."

"It must have been left behind in the crash," said David, "when your dad saw the lights. One of them crashed and must have laid eggs, and when they hatched, they killed the miners. Then they nearly killed us."

"And now they're gone," said Matthew.

"Now they're gone," agreed David. He looked at the sky. There seemed to be a faint, greenish glow behind the moon.

"I wonder if they're gone for good?" he asked.

"Go to sleep," said Matthew.

Cressy's Friend

The author

Lucy **Sussex**

talks about the story

"My last author's note earned me a letter to the editor, all about one little paragraph! So I'd rather not say anything. But I do want to thank David Wellington of Seattle, Washington, for the idea of crushing imaginary friends."

Cressy's Friend

Frelimo says to Cressy: "Someone's coming."

Cressy looks up from her video game, toward the front door. Her dad, busy ironing, sees the movement.

"Did Frelimo say who it is?" he asks Cressy.

She shakes her head, as if he had asked a stupid question.

The doorbell chimes, and Cressy's dad stands the iron up. He opens the door to reveal a well-dressed couple who look like government officials.

"Janice Walton, Department of Child Welfare." She prances into the room.

"And this is Dr. Jon Pearmain, one of our consultant psychologists."

Cressy's dad rolls his eyes and closes the door behind the visitors.

"They never sent you before," he says, staring at Janice Walton.

Frelimo says to Cressy: "Your dad thinks she's pretty cute."

Cressy giggles. The adults all turn and stare.

"And this," says Dr. Pearmain, "is Cressy, I presume."

He is looking at Cressy the way a cat looks at a mouse.

Cressy's dad gulps. "Tea?" he says quickly. "Coffee? Please excuse the mess, but I'm a single dad, and it's ironing day."

"We have read your file," says Dr. Pearmain. He sits down in an armchair, staring at Cressy.

Cressy stares unblinkingly back.

Frelimo says to Cressy: "You can stare him down. I'll help."

Two big, brown, adult eyes behind round, thick glasses stare into Cressy's pale blue eyes—brown against blue, a fight to the end. But then Cressy's dad comes between them, tray in hand.

"Your coffee," he says to Dr. Pearmain, who is rubbing his eyes. "Ms. Walton, your tea."

There are two cups of milk in front of Cressy.

"For you know who," Cressy's dad says brightly.

"We know," says Ms. Walton. "Cressy's little friend."

"Frelimo gets very angry when he doesn't get his milk," says Cressy.

"Like when he helped you with your math assignment, and the teacher gave you zero out of ten?" Ms. Walton says silkily.

"She hasn't been expelled," Cressy's dad says quickly. "Just suspended."

"But there is also the question of vandalism of a school computer."

Frelimo says to Cressy: "One and one doesn't equal two."

Cressy repeats it.

"I beg your pardon?" Ms. Walton says.

"That was what Frelimo said. One is the math assignment. Frelimo says he wasn't upset about that. He shouldn't have been using what you call cal . . ."

"Calculus," says Dr. Pearmain. "Very advanced math. That's why your teacher said you were cheating, Cressy."

"And the other one is the computer. Frelimo was only trying to improve it. They don't make two."

"She means there's no connection," says Cressy's dad. "I get these conversations all of the time. I can follow the logic."

"But it's not a normal child's logic," says Dr. Pearmain.

"How many normal children do you see?" asks Cressy's dad.

"Do you call using calculus at Cressy's age normal?"

"So, she's a bright girl. So, she has an imaginary

friend. So what! I had an imaginary friend at that age, too, though it wasn't green or tentacled."

He stops short. Cressy has stepped on his foot.

He laughs nervously. "I had a giant bunny rabbit, or so my mother tells me."

"Were you a gifted child?" asks Dr. Pearmain. "Recently, I've started to do some research on imaginary friends. It seems the children who have them are often highly intelligent."

Frelimo says to Cressy: "He knows about the others!"

Janice Walton butts in: "How did she do that?"

"Do what?"

"That second cup of milk just disappeared!"

"Don't worry about it," says Cressy's dad. "Happens all of the time."

"But I've been watching her."

"Cressy's a big fan of David Copperfield," says her dad. "You know, that magician on TV."

Cressy sighs. Her dad is a terrible liar.

"I see," says Dr. Pearmain. "A math genius and a magic whiz."

Frelimo says to Cressy: "Time for action!"

The iron suddenly shoots blue sparks across the room.

Frelimo says to Cressy: "Let's scram!"

Cressy's dad leaps up and runs into the kitchen, returning with a broom. Using the handle as a club, he pokes at the power switch, knocking over the ironing board.

Cressy and Frelimo sneak toward the front door.

The iron dangles in midair at the end of its electric cord. Then gravity pulls the plug from the outlet and the iron crashes to the floor.

Cressy actually has a hand on the doorknob when a voice says, "Excuse me!" Dr. Pearmain's big hand clamps down on hers. There's no escape now.

"Does *that* happen all of the time?" Janice Walton says to Cressy's dad.

He looks at Cressy.

"It wasn't me, Dad, it was Frelimo."

"We can't stay here," Dr. Pearmain says. "Not with dangerous electrical malfunctions. I think we'll continue this interview back at my office."

"I'm coming too," says Cressy's dad, with a glance at Ms. Walton.

Dr. Pearmain, still holding Cressy's hand tightly, opens the front door. Down the flight of stairs they go, heading toward a little red car. Dr. Pearmain almost has the passenger door open when something flies by his ear and smashes on the pavement.

"The neighbor's petunias," says Cressy's dad, as he gets in. "Never could stand 'em."

"Frelimo!" yells Cressy. She waves wildly as another potted plant falls to the ground.

"This place is vandal city!" Dr. Pearmain says. He starts the car, shaking so much that he nearly stalls as he pulls away from the curb.

Cressy says, "You left Frelimo behind. He'll be angry!"

She unbuckles her seat belt and kneels on the seat, looking through the rear window.

"Cressy, sit down!" says her dad.

"No," says Cressy. "Here comes Frelimo! He's sliding down the railings." She waves with both hands. "Now he's running down the path. Oh look, there's Josh from downstairs and his skateboard. Go, Frelimo, go!"

Dr. Pearmain glances into his rearview mirror and sees a boy in skating gear sprawled on the sidewalk. His skateboard is rolling by itself into the road. Dr. Pearmain speeds up, then slows down at the first of a line of speed bumps. Cressy bounces from the impact.

Her dad shouts, "Sit down and fasten your seat belt, or you'll go through the roof next!"

The skateboard is rolling down the center of the road as Dr. Pearmain makes a turn into a side street. Behind him, he sees a faint movement at the corner. Surely it can't be the skateboard?

Cressy has fastened her seat belt, but still looks anxiously back.

Dr. Pearmain can't believe it. It's that skateboard, skidding around the corner and racing after them. It must be a trick of the light.

"Yay, Frelimo!" shouts Cressy.

Ahead of them is the main road, divided by a

railroad crossing. As they near, bells ring, red lights flash, and the railroad gates begin to lower. In the rearview mirror the skateboard is closing in on the car. Dr. Pearmain floors the gas pedal. And the car shoots through the crossing, knocking off one arm of the lowering gate.

Behind them, the gate is down, and a siren hoots. They can hear the sound of a heavily loaded train, moving at high speed. Dr. Pearmain releases his breath. He is trapped behind a bus, which has stopped to let passengers on.

"Red lights won't stop Frelimo," Cressy says. "When he gets angry . . ."

They hear the thunder of the train, a sudden *whump!*, then the squealing of train brakes, sounding like fingernails on a blackboard. Cressy reaches for the door and jumps out. Dr. Pearmain turns off the engine and follows.

All three adults run, chasing Cressy back to the railroad crossing. When they catch up to her, she is standing at the gates, hands to her mouth. The freight train has finally stopped, having narrowly avoided derailment, for the rails have buckled beneath it. One grain car is half in, another half out of a deep hole that has suddenly opened beneath the tracks. Inside the hole is a bubbling, green ooze.

Cressy picks up a round, black object, a lost wheel from the skateboard. She clutches it tightly.

Her dad gapes. "And I thought Frelimo was just a result of Cressy playing too many computer games!"

"Frelimo was green, wasn't he?" says Janice Walton, faintly. "Whatever he was. And with tentacles, too."

Dr. Pearmain babbles, "I was only trying to carry out some research on imaginary friends to find out how these clever kids cope when they're lonely."

Cressy nods, pale but tearless. Then she puts her head to one side, as though listening to something faint and distant.

"Frelimo says he'll be back! And next time, he'll get *really* angry!"

So Sorry!

The author
Shannah Jay
talks about the story

"I love dogs, but maybe we trust them too much sometimes. When I let my imagination run free about what might happen, it leads me into all sorts of dark, horrible places. I hope this story doesn't turn you against real dogs!"

Shannah Jay

So Sorry!

"I'm not sorry!" Katie yelled, storming out of the house. She could hear her mother shouting, so she ran down the street. She hated school. It was boring. And she was not doing the dishes. It wasn't her turn.

Later, in the park, a dog walked up to her, trailing its leash. It wagged its tail and seemed to grin. She patted it, not at all frightened. Well, you wouldn't expect an alien to look like a yellow Labrador, would you?

Something stung her hand, and she tried to pull away, but she couldn't move. There was a humming sound inside her head.

When she did manage to move, she bent to pick up the leash, which scared her silly. She hadn't meant to do that. Something else was controlling her movements. And she hated it.

It took her another minute or two to realize she must have been drugged. By that time, she was walking along, holding the leash.

What was happening? She tried to drop the leash, but couldn't. She tried to stop walking and couldn't do that, either. And she couldn't say a word or call for help, no matter how hard she tried.

Fear trickled through her, as cold as ice melting down her back. This was just like a horror story. Only it was really happening to her. You never think something like this will happen to you. They're just stories, right?

Wrong! Bad things can happen to anyone. Only, by the time she realized that, it was too late.

A pair of sneakers came into sight, walking next to her. She glanced sideways. It was a boy, about her age, and he also had a dog on a leash.

He had a desperate look in his eyes. He moved his mouth, as if trying to speak, but no sound came out. She guessed then that he had been caught, too.

They turned into a driveway. It seemed like an ordinary house, but when the door swung open, there was no one in sight. She shivered as she walked inside and shivered again when the door slammed shut behind her.

The boy made a gurgling sound. Katie couldn't make any sound. If she could, she'd have been screaming.

Another door swung open, showing steps leading down into a cellar. The dog moved out of her way. The leash dropped from her hand. She started moving again.

Katie struggled to resist, but it was no use. All she could do was walk down into the darkness, her heart pounding. What now? Were they going to kill her? Who was doing this?

The boy walked behind her. She was glad he was there but was still terrified.

At the bottom were two seats, like dentist's chairs. They sat down. Straps slid across their bodies.

As the chairs tipped back, so that they were lying down, everything turned hazy.

When Katie awoke, she was lying on a bench. The boy was on another one next to her and there were about twenty other kids nearby. But they looked like they were asleep.

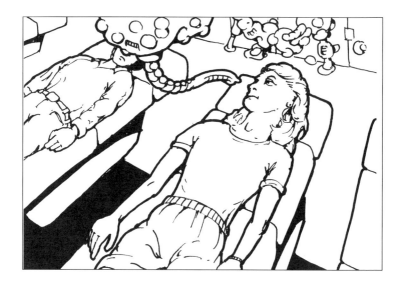

She tried to sit up but could only move her head.

The boy opened his eyes. "Where are we? What's going on?"

Katie found she could speak. "I don't know."

"Can you move?"

"Only my head. What's your name?"

"Jake."

"I'm Katie."

A tube dropped from the ceiling and wriggled toward her mouth.

"No!" She didn't want to be drugged or poisoned. But no matter how hard she tried, she couldn't move away, and when she shut her mouth, another gadget swung across and pried it open.

Water trickled between her lips. At least, she hoped it was water. She had to swallow it, or she would have choked.

The boy was in the same position, with a black tube in his mouth. His face looked angry and frightened. Well, who wouldn't be frightened? She was. She was terrified.

When the tubes slid away, she expected to fall asleep, but didn't. She looked at Jake. "What was that?"

"Water, I hope."

They talked. She told him about her family. He didn't have any brothers or sisters and lived with his grandma.

"She'll be worried."

"I'm worried," she admitted.

"Yeah. Me, too."

There was a chiming sound, then a pattering noise, and the dogs came into the room. They looked sort of fuzzy. As Katie watched, they began to change, growing taller.

Their front paws turned into hands. They were not like human hands, because they only had two fingers and a thumb.

And their faces had huge eyes and small mouths. No sign of a nose or ears. No hair, either.

"What are they?" whispered Jake.

"Aliens. They have to be. No Earth creature can change its shape." Suddenly she felt angry at the

way she'd been captured. She got angry sometimes. That's when she usually landed herself in trouble, like today. But she'd never been in such big trouble.

Before she could think, she shouted, "How dare you keep us here like this? Who do you think you are?"

The two creatures blinked their eyes and sounds came out of their mouths.

"What's going on here?" Jake said.

There was silence, then one creature said, "What's going on here?" in a voice just like Jake's.

"I don't like this at all," Katie whispered.

"I don't like this at all," the other creature whispered, in exactly her voice.

She and Jake exchanged shocked glances, then shut their mouths tight.

"We are sorry." The creature spoke slowly. "We must—find out—about your people."

Katie couldn't let that pass. "You don't have to capture us to do that! It's dumb! It'll make people angry." She held her breath. Had she upset them?

The creature's own voice sounded this time, thin, with an echo behind it. "Sadly, we must be very careful. We cannot risk showing ourselves yet."

Jake gave a snort. "Well, our people won't thank you for kidnapping us."

"They won't know."

There was silence while that horrible thought sank in. If no bodies were found, Katie's parents would never know what had happened to her. People disappeared all of the time.

"Who are those other kids? Did you kidnap them, too?" Jake jerked his head toward the unconscious bodies around them.

The others must have been from all over the world. They had different skin colors and clothes. They looked about the same age, though. They were in their early teens, like Katie and Jake.

The aliens didn't answer Jake's question. "We need you to stand up."

"Drop dead!" said Katie, still mad.

The benches moved into a slanted position. A cone of bright light shone down and the straps came undone. Katie gasped as she tumbled to the ground. The benches rolled out of sight.

On his knees beside her, Jake groaned. "My foot's asleep."

Katie was very stiff. They couldn't see the creatures because of the bright light. When they could stand, they moved close together for comfort.

Nothing happened.

"Can we escape?" she mouthed.

They tried to move through the light, but their bodies just bounced off it as if they'd hit a rubber wall.

"What are you doing to us?" Jake kicked the wall of light, but his foot bounced back, and he nearly fell over. "Ouch!"

Katie shivered. "I don't like this at all."

The light moved away. She walked across the bigger space. It was exactly five steps wide. "What is going on here?" she shouted.

There was no answer.

After a while, the light moved toward them again, pushing them with it, and the benches slid into view.

"Please lie down now," said one of those thin voices.

"No!" Katie tried to avoid her bench, but a metal arm shot out and closed around her wrist like a handcuff. It dragged her onto the bench. It felt terrible to be so helpless.

She turned toward Jake. Then she felt a sting in her arm and she fell down a long, black tunnel into sleep.

When she awoke, she was still on the bench. So it wasn't a nightmare. It was real. She felt like crying, or screaming, or both. But she saw Jake watching her and blinked away the tears.

"What now?" She even managed a grin—well, nearly.

"Who knows?" He looked pretty upset, too.

What happened next was even more terrifying. The two aliens came into the room. They stood by the benches and began to change shape until they looked a lot like Katie and Jake.

They just stood there, staring down at the two humans and changing things until they looked exactly like them.

Suddenly Katie realized what was happening. "They're going to take our places. That's why no one will know what happened to us."

Jake's expression was as horrified as hers.

She asked, "Are you going to kill us?"

The figure that looked like her went all blurry, then became clear again. It spoke in her voice, which definitely made her feel worse. "We do not kill."

"Then why did you capture us?" Jake yelled.

"We must borrow your shapes to learn about life here."

"Oh, yeah?" He glared at it. "And what do we do while you're with our families?"

"We take you away from this planet."

That was how Katie got to ride in a flying saucer. Yeah, and she hadn't even believed in them before. Well, she believed in them now, all right.

It helped to stay angry. Other kids were very quiet. Some tried to destroy things, but if you got violent, you just fell asleep.

Katie decided she'd rather stay awake, thank-you.

"I'll never pet a dog again," she muttered to Jake as the flying saucer drew near the big spaceship on the other side of the moon. They were strapped down again, but they could see what was happening on a huge screen.

"I don't think you'll ever get the chance." He swallowed hard. "I don't think we'll ever get back to Earth."

"So sorry," said one of those quiet whispering voices above their heads. "So very sorry you cannot go back."

That brought tears to Katie's eyes.

She wished suddenly that she could tell her mother she was sorry for getting into trouble at school. She'd even be glad to do the stupid dishes. Anything would be better than this.

"What good is being sorry?" she yelled. "You've stolen our lives."

"So very, very sorry . . ."

The big hatch of the spaceship opened and swallowed them up.

No one spoke as it closed behind them.

About the Illustrators

The Story Illustrator
Grant Gittus

Grant Gittus produces most of his artwork on computer. While he finds this creative and challenging, he says it lacks the artistic thrill of working with your hands on a piece of paper. He says **Thrillogy** gave him the chance to go back to doing what he loves doing best.

The Cover Illustrator
Marc McBride

Marc McBride has illustrated covers for several magazines and children's books. Marc currently creates the realistic images for his covers using acrylic ink with an airbrush. To solve his messy studio problem, he plans to use computer graphics instead.